WERNHER VON BRAUN

A Life from Beginning to End

BY HOURLY HISTORY

Table of Contents

Introduction

Wernher Magnus Maximilian von Braun was born on March 23, 1912, in Wirsitz—a town that today belongs to Poland but back then was part of Prussia, nestled within the greater German Empire. Wernher's lineage traces back to a long line of aristocratic landowners.

His father, Magnus von Braun, grew up on a sprawling estate near Königsberg in East Prussia. This was more than just a home; it was a sacred connection to the land and a symbol of his German identity. Magnus grew up in a society where aristocratic bloodlines were tied to military service, and his childhood was influenced by the traditions of the Prussian military, which emphasized discipline and loyalty. He eventually opted for a career in civil service and became involved in the government, working as an assistant to a trade minister.

In 1910, Magnus married Emmy von Quistorp, the daughter of another prominent landowner. Emmy herself came from a distinguished lineage. Her ancestry traced directly back to King Philippe III of France and Helen of Brunswick through Countess Irmgard de Rietberg, and it also connected her to

Waldemar the Great of Denmark through both Swedish and Danish lines. Furthermore, she was a descendant of King Robert III of Scotland and King Edward III of England.

Magnus and Emmy seemed to have a bright future ahead of them, and they welcomed their first child, a boy named Sigismund, in 1911. However, Magnus's career took a turn when he was assigned to the remote town of Wirsitz in Prussian Posen as a district magistrate. This rural posting was far from the glamorous social circles of Berlin and came with its own set of challenges. Wirsitz had a predominantly Polish population, which complicated Magnus's role as he navigated the tensions between the German administration and the people they ruled over. It was here that little Wernher would be born in 1912.

The upside of being far from any larger cities was that life in Wirsitz was relatively calm for the family during the years leading up to World War I. Magnus focused on his work and was often distant, while Emmy took care of their children. Wernher, who took after his mother, became a bit of a mystery to Magnus, especially as he grew older and started to show an interest in ideas that were not typically embraced by their conservative background.

Chapter One

Early Life in Prussia

"As a little boy, Wernher loved the piano and composed his own music. For a time we even thought he would make music his career. But it was not to be."

—Emmy von Quistorp von Braun

Just a couple of years after Wernher was born, World War I broke out. This supposed war to end all wars had the Central Powers of Germany, Austria-Hungary, Bulgaria, and the Ottoman Empire taking on much of the rest of the world. Why? Well, for starters, a Serbian nationalist made the fateful decision to assassinate the Austrian Archduke Franz Ferdinand when he was visiting the Balkans in June 1914. This incident triggered a series of events that pulled nations into the conflict as they rushed to support their allies, quickly escalating a local issue into a global war.

The von Brauns learned about the assassination from their chauffeur just a day after it happened. A month later, with over a million Russian troops mobilizing to the east, Magnus took on his role as a German mobilization officer. For many Germans, there was a real excitement about the war, which they viewed as a defensive action against Czarist Russia. However, for Emmy, this was a particularly scary time. She was acutely aware of how vulnerable Magnus was as part of the German government. Their young boys, though they might not fully grasp what was happening, were still at an age where they could feel the tension at home. That sense of danger would stick with them, even if they couldn't quite articulate it yet.

Things took a turn in November when Russian forces moved toward Posen and Silesia after pushing back the German troops from Warsaw. They would soon be threatening Wirsitz directly. In response, Magnus sent Emmy on a risky journey to Berlin. She was to bring three million marks from the local bank in Wirsitz and deposit it into a bank in Berlin to safeguard it during the fighting. It took her two days to get there and two days to get back, but she successfully completed her mission.

Even though danger was close, Magnus decided to keep his family in Wirsitz. He knew that if word got out that his wife and sons were fleeing the region, it would send the townsfolk—many of whom didn't even view themselves as German in the first place—into a frenzy of panic. Instead, Emmy helped to set up a military hospital that quickly filled with wounded soldiers, and Magnus focused on drilling young reservists. Their two young sons were meanwhile taken care of by servants. By spring 1915, however, Magnus was transferred to a more prestigious role in the government in Berlin. The family would spend the rest of the war in the German capital.

Of course, in 1918, Germany ended up losing the war and, with it, a good chunk of its territory. At the signing of the infamous Treaty of Versailles, Posen—and the town of Wirsitz—was part of the territory that was lost. In addition, the treaty stipulated that Germany would have to pay a staggering $5 billion in war debts. Many in Germany were deeply dismayed. The defeat was not only a blow to national esteem but also a blow to their finances, as the German economy took a tumble. Indeed, it was in the pocketbook that most Germans were hit the most severely.

This humiliating loss became the backdrop of Wernher von Braun's childhood. Perhaps it was this failed political reality right in front of him that first caused Wernher to look upwards instead of outwards. The imagery right in front of his eyes was too painful, so he preferred to look up at the clouds instead and to dream what might lay beyond them in that dark void we call outer space. Nations and their arbitrary borders are rather trivial when one considers the big picture, and Wernher most certainly did dream of one day accomplishing something bigger than nation-states and principalities, something that would fundamentally alter all of humanity. It was as a child in post-war Germany that Wernher von Braun first learned to reach for the stars.

Chapter Two

First Forays into Rocketry

"The wagon was wholly out of control and trailing a comet's tail of fire, but my rockets were performing beyond my wildest dreams. Finally, they burned themselves out with a magnificent thunderclap and the vehicle rolled to a halt. The police took me into custody very quickly. Fortunately, no one had been injured, so I was released in charge of the Minister of Agriculture—who was my father."

—Wernher von Braun

As a child, Wernher von Braun was expected to study, work hard, and seek to lead an otherwise honorable life. Wernher certainly didn't disappoint. On the contrary, he quickly showed a keen ability to excel in just about any field he applied himself to. He was eager, studious, and had an insatiable curiosity. It was this curiosity that had him asking a whole lot of questions. His teachers were amazed at his seemingly insatiable appetite for knowledge. For the most part, instructors are thrilled to find students who actually take an interest in what they are teaching. Wernher von Braun, however, was soon asking questions which even his teachers were hard-pressed to find the answers to.

The young Wernher also turned out to be a great musician. During his early years, in fact, he proved to be something of a child prodigy. He was so prodigious on the piano and the cello that, for a time, he seriously considered a career in music. Wernher von Braun even took some lessons from the great composer Paul Hindemith. The fact that he even had access to Paul Hindemith is, of course, an indication of the great connections that his parents had. He continued to pursue music with a passion, and as an adolescent, he penned a few original piano compositions of his own. Nevertheless, it was the stars that would ultimately call Wernher von Braun.

By 1920, the von Brauns were back in Berlin after having spent about a year in the East Prussian town of Gumbinnen. It was a wild and heady time for Germany. After the war, the German government had collapsed to give rise to the Weimer Republic—Germany's first experiment with democracy. Prior to this, the German state was being run as an autocracy. Wilhelm II, Germany's *kaiser*, had ruled by dictate. Now, Germans were being introduced to the notion of government by the people. But not everyone liked the changes that were coming to Germany.

After the war, jazz, drunkenness, and high culture flourished. Foreign writers, artists, and musicians were suddenly flocking to the German capital of Berlin. Some were excited at these cultural developments, but others looked on in dismay, feeling as if an alien influence was seeking to change German society. Wernher von Braun was just a child during this period, but even as he got older, he was never all that interested in such things. Political and social movements didn't mean much to him. Like many from his wealthy, upper-class background, it was considered beneath him to be engaged in the social changes that were often ignited by the lower classes. This detachment would later prove to be a dangerous blind spot as the frustrations of disaffected Germans paved the way for the rise of Nazi tyranny.

Wernher's family were, of course, firmly against the move from an autocratic to a democratic style of governance. In fact, it was Magnus's support of an attempted coup to bring down the Weimar Republic and restore an autocratic government that had cost him his governmental job in Gumbinnen. After moving to Berlin, he instead took up a job as a bank director. Yet the von Braun family's many connections would soon come in handy again, and any previous setbacks wouldn't stop Magnus from being involved in the government again. By 1924, he was handed the post of Reichsminister of Agriculture. Magnus von Braun would stay on at this post all the way until 1932, during the last fitful years of Paul von Hindenburg's presidency.

As good of a student as Wernher von Braun was, it was during these years that he first received a dent in his academic armor. Wernher's grades in mathematics and physics had begun to slip. He was distracted by a new passion: rocketry and the theory of manned spaceflight. Wernher had been fascinated by space for as long as he could remember, but the year 1924 had him making his first attempts to launch some rockets of his own. He was only 12 years old at the time and was eager to see what a bit of rocketry could do. His first experiments involved nothing more than purchasing some run-of-the-mill fireworks and setting them off.

Fireworks have been around since they were invented several centuries ago in ancient China and are indeed a rudimentary form of rocket. Wernher likely figured that such well-known variations of rocketry were the most logical place to start. So it was that he purchased his first rockets and began setting them off. He sent them aloft alright; the only trouble was when they came back down. It's said that one hit a fruit stand, and the other bulldozed into a bakery. Needless to say, neither the vendors nor their patrons were too happy with little Wernher von Braun. Worse was yet to come, however, when Wernher truly began to experiment with his rockets.

Wernher was indeed rather inventive and not just content to launch rockets into the air. Instead, he began to try and use them in a multitude of other ways. In particular, he decided to attach them to the sides of his play wagon. Yes indeed, just imagine Wernher von Braun inside a kid's classic pull wagon with a rocket attached to each side. Wernher then had some local kids push the wagon right into one of the main roads that led to downtown Berlin. The kids lit the fuse of the rocket, and Wernher was off! He didn't exactly launch himself to the Moon, but he did manage to end up at the local police station.

The rocket wagon, it turns out, had sent Wernher von Braun slamming into a fruit stand. This was a pretty serious incident, but considering Wernher's young age, his apologetic nature, and his father's prominent position, he was essentially let off with a stern warning. He was told not to engage in any more risky endeavors with rockets. With a policeman staring him down, Wernher of course agreed to do just that. His mother also had her own bit of advice. She suggested that it was best to avoid such risky situations since the world could benefit from a living scientist much more than one killed in a rocket crash. Wernher von Braun couldn't help but agree.

Chapter Three

Struggles in School

"For my confirmation, I didn't get a watch and my first pair of long pants, like most Lutheran boys. I got a telescope. My mother thought it would make the best gift. I became an amateur astronomer, which led to my interest in the universe, which led to my curiosity about the vehicle which will one day carry a man to the Moon."

—Wernher von Braun

In 1925, Wernher von Braun was sent away to a prestigious boarding school. The school itself was situated in the rather elegant Ettersburg Castle, just outside of the city of Weimar in what was then the Free State of Thuringia. Wernher was sent here by his parents, largely to keep their son—already known for his penchant for rocketry—out of trouble. The school had a rather strict schedule, which had students plugging away for six hours straight on their coursework before allowing them to pursue other interests in the afternoon. Even their free time in the afternoon had to be spent on things that were deemed to be constructive activities. Rather than just having fun, students learned skilled trades such as woodwork or farming.

Just prior to his arrival, Wernher von Braun's mother had gifted him with a telescope. This would prove to be crucial, for Wernher would make his afternoon pursuit that of looking to the stars. The school itself was apparently quite alright with him pursuing the craft of astronomy, and it became a real passion for him. It was perhaps this moment of looking to the stars that inspired Wernher to seek to shoot his rockets toward those great stellar bodies. These desires were further cemented when von Braun began to read science fiction magazines, which dared to imagine what it might be like if space travel were possible. He was an avid fan of classic science fiction novelists H. G. Wells and Jules Verne, who dared to dream of practical methods to make such a reality.

During his time at the school, von Braun also came across a book entitled *By Rocket into Planetary Space*, which had come out in 1923. The book was written by the man who would come to be known as the father of rocketry,

Hermann Oberth. Oberth's aspirations and the technical details he shared captivated Wernher von Braun, and as such, he began to consider how rockets could be used to take people to outer space. Wernher, in fact, dreamed of making that trip himself. In the end, of course, Wernher von Braun didn't become an astronaut, but he did become the mastermind behind America's space program, which not only sent America's first astronauts into space but also to the surface of the Moon. But before von Braun could do any of this, he first needed to conquer his greatest foe: mathematics.

By the time that he enrolled at the boarding school, Wernher's grades in mathematics and physics had begun to slip. He never really liked math, but he was becoming increasingly aware that his poor math ability was holding him back. He realized that professional scientists didn't do their work ad-hoc and simply guess at things like fuel quantities or trajectories. He realized that in order to be a professional rocket scientist, he had to be precise. He needed to be able to rely upon a solid understanding of mathematical calculations.

From that day forward, he turned his attention to not just churning out passing grades in his math class but to developing an understanding of mathematics that would surpass his classmates and even most of his instructors. Considering how poorly Wernher von Braun initially performed in mathematics, the fact that he overcame this weak spot is a testament to his perseverance. As soon as he realized he needed math to achieve his dreams, he poured himself into the subject and became one of the best math students one could ever imagine.

Wernher was so good, in fact, that he found himself needing more rigorous training. He outgrew his old school and began asking his father to allow him to transfer to the Hermann Lietz school in the North Sea. This boarding school was nestled in Spiekeroog Island, located just off Germany's northern coast. Wernher arrived at the school in 1928.

It was apparently after he got a good handle on his mathematics that he managed to convince the administrators at the school to spend cool, hard cash for his new pursuit of astronomy. He requested that they raise money for a new telescope so that he and other students could better calculate the distance between the stars. The fact that Wernher von Braun was successful in pitching his case for this investment has often been cited as the start of a lifelong pattern of convincing corporations and governmental entities to finance his ambitious (and often expensive) projects.

Wernher von Braun was no slacker on his end of the bargain and proved to be an excellent student—so excellent, in fact, that when his mathematics teacher suffered a health crisis, Wernher was tapped to replace them. He was just a student, but he didn't shirk away from the responsibility. Wernher von Braun threw himself into the task headlong. He was able to clearly demonstrate to the other students the best way forward for them to learn, and his ability to reach them was evident by way of the fact that every single student von Braun took under his wing passed with flying colors.

Chapter Four

The VfR: Meeting Willy Ley

"I don't remember the name of the magazine or author, but the article described an imaginary trip to the Moon. It filled me with a romantic urge. Interplanetary travel! Here was a task worth dedicating one's life to! Not just to stare through a telescope at the Moon and the planets, but to soar through the heavens and actually explore the mysterious universe!"

—Wernher von Braun

It was after he had conquered mathematics and graduated from the Hermann Lietz school that an 18-year-old Wernher von Braun headed off to the Charlottenburg Institute of Technology in Berlin. He met a lot of interesting and life-long friends in Berlin, including that of fellow rocket man Willy Ley.

Ley later recalled his first encounter with Wernher von Braun quite clearly. He came home one day to find von Braun at the family piano, pummeling the keys with a passionate rendition of *Moonlight Sonata* by Beethoven. It's perhaps fitting that the man who was determined to send a man to the Moon played a rather exquisite variation of *Moonlight Sonata*. Ley was impressed with von Braun's musical ability and, upon striking up a conversation with him, was equally impressed with his impeccable grace and social manners. He was a child of high society in Germany, and he obviously carried himself as such, marking him as someone who would likely move well in the higher social circles of the day.

But what was the reason that this young man with impeccable manners and piano skills had come to visit Ley's home? Ley soon found out. Wernher had learned through his own already growing social circles that Willy Ley was part of an amateur rocket group known as the *Verein für Raumschiffahrt*, or as it would translate into English, Society for Space Travel. As the group gained steam, they simply called themselves "VfR."

Still thrilled by all things rockets and all things space, Wernher von Braun wanted to join the club. Although this group was indeed a bunch of amateurs, they were truly dedicated to the cause. The group first got its start in 1927 and, since then, did everything they could to try and further their aims. They were so serious that early on, they established their own official charter. The two main aims of the group were to generate a deep and profound interest in space travel while experimenting with and building new and exciting rockets that might one day take people there.

Through his membership with the VfR, Wernher soon came into contact with his childhood hero, Hermann Oberth. Oberth, who was preparing a rocketry exhibit in Berlin at the time, noticed Wernher's enthusiasm and invited him to help. Wernher dedicated every free moment to assisting Oberth with the setup. When the exhibit opened, Wernher von Braun was there, exuding confidence as he answered questions with the poise of an expert. Travel to the Moon is just around the corner, he confidently proclaimed to anyone who would listen.

The first major development for the VfR came later in 1930, when Ley and von Braun managed to get the green light from the German military to utilize an abandoned ammunition dump in the Berlin suburb of Reinickendorf. The

VfR renamed the joint *Raketenflugplatz*, or Rocket Launch Site, and immediately got to work. At last, with their own proving grounds, they were able to experiment with relative abandon. They even turned abandoned buildings on the site into storage units and office parks. During their first year at the site, the group is said to have conducted some 87 launches, as well as tested out a wide variety of rocket motors.

Even while the VfR rolled up their sleeves and got to work, Wernher von Braun continued his education. In 1931, he ended up spending a term studying at the Federal Institute of Technology in Zurich, Switzerland. Here, he befriended an American student by the name of Constantine Generales. Constantine would long remember Wernher and would later recall just how serious he was about space travel. At the time, it was considered almost a ridiculous concept by most. Go to the Moon? That's absurd! The very notion of traveling to the Moon back then seemed more akin to something from the funny pages than any serious academic pursuit.

Nevertheless, there was Wernher von Braun preaching the virtues of manned space flight. This meant that he had to consider not just rocketry but all aspects of spaceflight. His hero

Hermann Oberth had already tackled some of the concepts, envisioning a rudimentary spacesuit for space pilots so that they could breathe without any difficulties. Wernher von Braun likewise plumbed the depths of such concepts and explored the possibilities. Leaving nothing to chance, he sought to understand what the effect of leaving the Earth's protective atmosphere might have on the organs of the body, especially as it pertained to undergoing severe stresses such as the g-forces that riding on a rocket would undoubtedly unleash.

Since his new American friend Constantine Generales was in Zurich studying medicine, Wernher von Braun regularly bombarded him with a litany of medical questions about what space travel might do to the human body. Generales didn't have answers to all of von Braun's questions, but he did recommend that animals should be sent to space before anyone dared send human beings into such an unpredictable and potentially hostile environment. Considering as much, it's worth noting that this is indeed exactly what subsequent, early space programs did. The Russians famously sent a dog named Laika into orbit in 1957, and the Americans launched a monkey into subspace in 1948, on board one of Wernher von Braun's own V-2 rockets no less.

At any rate, it was Constantine Generales who helped Wernher von Braun engage in some of his first experiments to learn what g-forces might do to astronauts. They constructed a crude centrifuge consisting of a bicycle wheel attached horizontally to the top of a table. Containers were hooked up to the side of the wheel, and mice were put in them. The wheel was then sent spinning, and the mice were sent along for the ride.

The first thing Constantine and Wernher observed upon stopping the wheel was the obvious distress of the mice. Their hearts were beating out of their chests, and they were certainly scared. After the mice were euthanized and dissected, an even clearer picture emerged. Von Braun and Generales were able to document what the g-forces of the centrifuge had done to the mice. The mice suffered from bleeding in the brain and even the entire displacement of organs. Hearts and lungs had been literally shoved out of place after sustaining the g-forces of being locked inside that spinning wheel. It was this kind of data that helped Wernher von Braun better understand what the g-forces of space flight might do to human pilots and how such effects could be mitigated.

As groundbreaking as this work might have been at the time, not everyone appreciated it. Von Braun's landlady was particularly aghast when she discovered little splatters of mouse blood all over her apartment. He was ordered to cease and desist at once. Nevertheless, Wernher von Braun got the data he needed, and soon, even more opportunities would emerge.

Chapter Five

Joining the German Army

I had been struck during my casual visits to Reinickendorf by the energy and shrewdness with which this tall, fair young student with the broad massive chin went to work, and by his astonishing theoretical knowledge. . . . When General Becker later decided to approve our army establishment for liquid-propellant rockets, I put Wernher von Braun first on my list of proposed technical assistants.

—Captain Walter Dornberger

In the spring of 1932, Wernher von Braun graduated from the Institute of Technology in Berlin with a degree in mechanical engineering. He was happy with his degree, but he openly wondered if it was enough. Wernher began to consider that a traditional degree in engineering was not quite up to par with what would actually be needed for sustained, manned space flight.

It was in his quest to improve his own understanding that he began to turn to physics for answers. He enrolled himself at the Friedrich-Wilhelm University of Berlin and pursued a degree in doctoral studies. He earned his PhD in physics in 1934. Big changes were taking place in Germany in the meantime, with the rise of Adolf Hitler and the Nazi Party. Hitler was elected as chancellor of Germany in 1933 under President Paul von Hindenburg and was subsequently made the supreme leader of Germany a short time later.

True to his nature, Wernher von Braun didn't concern himself much with the latest political happenings in Germany. His only concern was getting funding and support to continue his research. As such, as the Nazi Party gained prominence, he felt it was only natural for him to consult with the power brokers of the regime in order to ensure that his experiments into the field of rocketry and potential space flight could continue. This is not so much an excuse for von Braun's actions as it is an explanation.

It was this cold, cut-and-dry logic that led Wernher von Braun first to become a civilian employee of the German Army in 1932 and later an official member of the Nazi Party in 1937. For Wernher, he viewed becoming a member of the most prominent party in Germany as merely a means to open doors for his research. He knew that without consulting with these Nazi gatekeepers first, his work would likely go nowhere. It seems he was willing to look past some of the more unsavory aspects of the Nazi regime if it meant he could continue to work on his passion project.

But even though Wernher von Braun was seeking a means to achieve space flight, the Germans were already looking toward rockets as potential weapons of war. This push began back in 1929 when German Army Captain Walter Dornberger suggested the use of rockets as a way to circumvent the Treaty of Versailles that had been signed at the end of World War I. The treaty sought to significantly limit the German Army and minimize the buildup of potential munitions. But since the treaty only stipulated limits on what was then considered conventional weaponry, it said nothing at all about rockets.

To Dornberger, this omission appeared to be a loophole that could be exploited, and he was eager to take advantage of it. He was given the green light by the German Army to go ahead and try to find military applications for liquid-fuel rockets. Dornberger established a team at a proving grounds south of Berlin and engaged in a series of experiments with rockets.

While Dornberger was dedicated to the cause, he wasn't always the most careful with his work. It's said that on one occasion, he impatiently disassembled a rocket with a steel hammer and chisel rather than the copper tools that would otherwise be recommended. Sparks from the tools managed to send thousands of tiny black-powder particles into Dornberger's face. He would spend the better part of a year visiting military hospitals to remove the many particles one by one. Despite the pain and injury he sustained, Dornberger proved that he was dedicated to the cause and persevered.

Wernher von Braun and his team, in the meantime, managed to develop special aluminum walls that would have coolant run through the combustion chamber, thereby reducing temperature and mitigating the potential for explosive reactions. It was after Dornberger got wind of these developments that he extended von Braun a contract with the army. Wernher had a subsequent interview with a certain Colonel Karl Becker, who was in charge of the Army Weapons Office. The two men quickly hit it off, and von Braun was given a post directly with the army for rocket research and development in 1932.

The VfR meanwhile faced some problems of its own. First, the recently reconstituted German Air Force, the *Luftwaffe*, had been demanding to use the proving grounds at Reinickendorf for their drills. The next blow came when the VfR was suddenly hit with an outrageous utility bill. In Germany, inflation had been driving everything through the roof, but this bill was truly astronomical due to a set of leaky pipes that had been driving up the expenditure of water. As a result, the group had to cut ties with the Rocket Launch Site at Reinickendorf entirely in what seemed like a devastating setback.

Its former star, Wernher von Braun, couldn't complain too much since, at 21 years of age, he was now firmly embedded with the German Army and all the resources at its disposal. These resources included an Ordinance Department research grant he was awarded in 1933. During this period, one of the first breakthroughs achieved was the development of a liquid propellant motor, which utilized ethyl alcohol and liquid oxygen. Wernher von Braun's days spent testing this apparatus had him armed with a so-called igniter—basically a long wooden pole with gasoline at one end, which was used to ignite the rockets. His days largely consisted of shouting out the orders of *"Feuer! Benzin! Sauerstoff!"* In other words, "Fire! Gasoline! Oxygen!"

He wasn't achieving space flight yet, but the higher his rockets went aloft, with each and every launch, the closer he felt he was getting to one day reaching the stars. There were, of course, plenty of setbacks along the way. There were rockets that exploded upon the launch pad and miscalculations that sent them dangerously off course. Wernher von Braun knew that he was in for a steep learning curve, but he was all in.

These early tests led to the Aggregat rocket, or as it was otherwise known, the A-1. The A-1 was the first truly substantial prototype rocket that Wernher von Braun worked on. The goal for the A-1 was to create a reliable rocket launch system that could get the rocket aloft and keep it on a generally predictable flight path. Considering all the previous mishaps, this was most certainly not an easy task to accomplish. One of the first great innovations of this prototype was the inclusion of a gyroscopic spin in the nose section of the rocket. This was to help control the way that the rocket spun while in flight.

It was not enough to stabilize the A-1, however, and soon its design was scrapped in favor of a different one. The biggest problem, it was realized rather belatedly, was that the A-1 did not have proper fins. Wernher von Braun had to accept that attaching fins to the rocket—much like ancient tribes attached feathers to arrows— would do much to stabilize the flight path. This acknowledgment led to the creation of the A-2 rocket.

Along with fins, von Braun also took the extra step of moving the gyroscopic spin from the nose of the rocket down to its midsection. He found that this lessened the top-heaviness of the rocket and added even further stability to its flight. Wernher von Braun and his team were slowly but surely making progress.

Chapter Six

Meeting Hitler

"I was officially demanded to join the National Socialist Party. At this time, I was already Technical Director at the Army Rocket Center at Peenemunde. The technical work carried out there had, in the meantime, attracted more and more attention in higher levels. Thus, my refusal to join the party would have meant that I would have to abandon the work of my life. Therefore, I decided to join."

—Wernher von Braun

Wernher von Braun was a busy man in the 1930s, and along with perfecting his rockets, by 1935, he was tapped by the Luftwaffe to begin research into prototypes for the rocket-powered propulsion of planes. This was right up Wernher von Braun's alley since he had been interested in as much ever since he was a small child. Yes indeed, ever since he dared to strap a pair of rockets to the side of his childhood wagon, he had been dreaming of the day that rockets could give an extra boost to human transportation. And now, none other than the German Luftwaffe was encouraging him to look into the matter.

Wernher von Braun, who had recently become a licensed pilot himself, even tested some of the prototypes firsthand. It was a daring thing for him to do, but he did indeed successfully fly some early rocket-powered plane prototypes. It was just as the research and development of all these new prototypes were gaining speed, however, that Wernher and his team came to realize that they needed to procure more open space to perfect them. The ideal locale would be somewhere along a coastline so that rockets could be shot safely over water, thereby minimizing any potential damage when they came back down. It was actually while von Braun was on leave, paying a visit to his parents during Christmas in 1935, that his parents back home suggested a place called Peenemunde.

Peenemunde was an isolated swathe of land where Wernher's grandfather used to go duck hunting. They felt that it would provide just the type of proving grounds that the military was looking for. Von Braun himself subsequently visited the area, and he couldn't have agreed more. The site was located on a stretch of remote coastline on the Baltic Sea, some 150 miles (250 kilometers) north of Berlin. Peenemunde's widespread sand dunes and soft marshy terrain seemed to be a perfect natural cushion for falling debris.

Von Braun informed Dornberger of what he had discovered, and he was equally enthusiastic. They then sought out permission from the military top brass. Ultimately, it was General Albert Kesselring, the head of aircraft construction, who gave the green light, and the site of Peenemunde was acquired for official use. Peenemunde was a wilderness of raw land at this point, so it would take some time to transform it into a world-class research and development hub. But not that much time.

Between 1936 and 1939, an incredible effort was made by way of chopping down trees, digging up roots, and flattening the earth to shape and mold that rough terrain into suitable grounds for the site. Along with prepping the ground, important structures were built, such as test stands, barracks, bunkers, wind tunnels, and even a power plant. It was here that a wide variety of rockets would be tested and fired, but to von Braun's chagrin, the end goal was not initially space flight; on the contrary, these tests resulted in some of the most terrible and vengeful weapons of World War II.

The real turning point seems to have occurred in the spring of 1936 with the development of the A-4. This was the first rocket that Wernher von Braun constructed with specific performance specs in mind. He had done so under some rather alarming threats from his head honcho, Dornberger. At this stage in his career, Dornberger had made it quite clear to Wernher von Braun that the German Army would only continue to fund his projects if he got results. If he proved unable to demonstrate the military application for rockets, his project could be cut, and he would lose all the funding he had received.

Wernher certainly didn't want that, so he began to refashion his rockets as true weapons of war, considering them more akin to artillery than potential spacecraft. As such, he was thinking more along the lines of targeting and range. He wanted to demonstrate to his superior officers that he could extend the range of the rockets so that they could better target enemy forces. This involved a lot of new calculations as it pertained to such things as velocity, thrust, and navigation.

Wernher von Braun may not have agreed with all the politics that were afoot in Germany, but his research was becoming increasingly wedded to the German military. The German military, in turn, was being increasingly appropriated by Hitler and his Nazis. Any allusion otherwise was ultimately shattered when Hitler himself came to pay a visit on March 23, 1939, to check on Wernher von Braun and his team's progress.

Not too interested in Wernher von Braun's academic explanations of how rockets worked, Hitler's chief concern was over what kind of munitions the rockets could carry. He clearly wanted to use them to inflict maximum damage on Germany's perceived foes. To this fateful question, Hitler was informed that the current rockets did not have a payload to carry powerful warheads. Wernher's team was quick to point out, however, that with an increase in funding, they would be able to do so.

Hitler did not promise to increase funding at this point. Wernher and company would have to wait. It was quite clear that Wernher von Braun's continued development of his rockets very much depended upon the generous purse strings of his Nazi backers.

Chapter Seven

The Vengeance Weapons

"Science does not have a moral dimension. It is like a knife. If you give it to a surgeon or a murderer, each will use it differently."

—Wernher von Braun

After Germany's invasion of Poland in September 1939, which ignited the Second World War, Hitler himself began to openly speak of a secret weapons project that was in development. It seems that he finally saw the potential value in rocketry, and suddenly, Wernher von Braun and his team received the funding they had been looking for. It would take some time, but by 1942, the A-4 was complete and ready for service in the German armed forces. It was this rocket that would be the first of a long line of Hitler's so-called "vengeance weapons," which were largely used to bombard Great Britain.

By this point, Wernher von Braun had been made an honorary member of Nazi henchman Heinrich Himmler's dreaded paramilitary group, the SS. Von Braun later downplayed all of this as merely him seeking to curry favor with the top brass so that he could continue to receive funding for his research into rocketry. There is only one known photograph of Wernher wearing his SS uniform—one when he was standing behind Himmler himself. Von Braun claimed that this was the one and only time he wore the uniform. These claims were later disputed by others, however, who insisted that they witnessed Wernher von Braun sporting the uniform much more frequently than that. In 2002, in fact, a surviving SS officer claimed that Wernher regularly wore the uniform to official meetings.

At any rate, in 1943, when the A-4 was converted into use as one of Hitler's vengeance weapons, it became known as the V-2 (or *Vergeltungswaffe 2*, meaning "Vengeance Weapon 2"). The British, who were the prospective targets of this vengeance, had gotten wind of the program and launched an air raid on Peenemunde on August 17, 1943. The bombing caused extensive damage and killed 735 people—most of whom were forced laborers, but one was a chief engine designer by the name of Walter Thiel. This certainly set the program back and managed to delay the first deployment of the V-2s against Britain. Yet although the rocket program was delayed, it wasn't thwarted as the Allied had hoped.

In the fall of 1944, the V-2s began to rain down on Britain. It was a laborious effort to get these rockets off the assembly line and up into the air, and unfortunately enough, by this time, most of it was accomplished by way of slave labor. Inmates from concentration camps were used to construct the rockets in factories such as Mittelwerke, an underground site built into the Harz Mountains in southern Germany. Many died in the process—in fact, it's been said that more people died constructing the V-2 rockets than were actually killed by them in combat.

Although Wernher von Braun didn't spend much time in these factories himself, he did visit them several times. He said later, "The working conditions there were absolutely horrible. I saw the Mittelwerke several times, once while these prisoners were blasting new tunnels in there in what was a pretty hellish environment." Prisoners, many of whom were Jews or prisoners of war, were forced to work under grueling conditions, with little food, harsh punishments, and many dying from exhaustion, mistreatment, or disease.

We now know that von Braun never protested against the use of slave labor or the brutal treatment of the inmates. After the war, his involvement with the use of forced labor became a source of significant controversy. Although von Braun claimed he was unaware of the extent of the cruelty (especially at the concentration camps which he claimed never to have visited), there is considerable debate about how much he knew and to what degree he turned a blind eye to the horrors happening under the Nazi regime. Of course, as some of Wernher von Braun's colleagues were quick to point out, he was under the Nazi boot just as much as anyone else, and if he so much as made one idle protest, he would have likely been imprisoned or executed.

Wernher von Braun did indeed eventually get on the bad side of the Nazis. He was tattled on by an SS spy, who overheard him complaining about being forced to make weapons rather than spaceships. Wernher also made the mistake of complaining about the war effort, remarking that he felt the war was lost. The spy reported all of this back to her SS handlers, and Wernher von

Braun was promptly arrested for being a so-called "defeatist." The Nazi totalitarian state could not tolerate anyone who deviated from the Nazi script. Learning that Wernher was not so enthusiastic was deemed treasonous. Out of fear that he might even defect to Britain and take all his technical knowledge with him, von Braun was locked up behind bars.

Chapter Eight

Operation Paperclip: Move to the US

"Science and religion are not antagonists. On the contrary, they are sisters. While science tries to learn more about the creation, religion tries to better understand the creator. While through science man tries to harness the forces of nature around him, through religion he tries to harness the force of nature within him."

—Wernher von Braun

Wernher von Braun was arrested by the dreaded Nazi secret police—the Gestapo—in March 1944. He was placed in a Gestapo prison in Poland for two straight weeks without anyone even informing him what the exact charges leveled against him were. Unlike other nations, which guarantee prisoners certain rights, such as being informed of what crimes they committed, the Nazi regime did not extend any such courtesy. Wernher was left to languish in a prison cell, having no idea what he was charged with and whether he would ever see the light of day again. It took Dornberger to bail him out, along with another high-profile friend—Albert Speer—who was serving as the head of munitions and war production at the time. Together, they managed to convince Hitler that the program was too important to keep von Braun locked up, and so he was reinstated.

However, Wernher von Braun's previous assessment of Germany's losing trajectory was soon proven correct. That fateful summer of 1944, the Allied forces launched their famous D-Day invasion on the beaches of Normandy, and by the spring of 1945, they were heading straight for Berlin. Even more pressing for von Braun and his colleagues was the rapidly approaching Soviet Army coming from the east. The Germans had waged a brutal war against their Soviet enemies on the Eastern Front, and the Russians were eager for revenge. Wernher and company had likely already heard plenty of stories of Russian brutality against captured German soldiers. As such, Wernher and his colleagues decided that if they were to be captured, they would be better off being captured by the Americans rather than the Russians.

Wernher von Braun gathered together his staff and had them relocate with him to central Germany in a bid to meet the Americans advancing from the west. It was a chaotic period, and during one rather abrupt trip by car that March, von Braun was in a bad accident that shattered the bones of his left arm and shoulder. It was for this reason that when the Allied troops caught up with him that May, he was discovered with his arm in a cast. The doctors who had operated on him actually recommended that he stay put in the hospital to recover, but Wernher knew that he had to stay one step ahead of not just the Russians but also the SS.

In these final days, as everything was coming undone, there was still the danger of being targeted by the Nazi state. Just prior to Hitler's suicide on April 30, 1945, in fact, he had issued orders to have the rocket team liquidated and their technical files destroyed, lest they fall into enemy hands. Wernher von Braun got wind of this, and he and his inner circle of technicians fled by train to Austria, where they managed to finally meet up with advancing American forces on May 2. As it turns out, the top brass of the US military were already looking for him. They were well aware of the top scientists of Germany, and Wernher von Braun was at the top of their list of big brains to bag. This effort to grab up the best and brightest minds of Germany would later be dubbed Operation Paperclip.

After it was all said and done, Wernher von Braun and his colleagues would end up at Fort Bliss in El Paso, Texas, where they would be put to work developing the same designs they had fashioned for the *Führer* for the United States of America. It wasn't exactly an easy transition for von Braun to make. Back in Germany, he had a whole team of engineers and other technicians at his beck and call. Now, he was made subservient to a young army major by the name of James Hamill, who didn't seem to be too thrilled about Wernher von Braun or his work with rocketry.

It was perhaps his discomfort and a longing for home that had Wernher seek out his first cousin Maria Louise von Quistorp for marriage. He began a long-distance correspondence before getting leave to briefly join her in Germany, where the two were married in the spring of 1947. He was 35 years old at the time, while she was only 18. This union eventually produced three children: Iris, Margrit, and Peter.

Upon his return stateside, Wernher von Braun sought to change his fortunes. He requested more resources to be able to continue his research but seemed to be stifled at every turn. It was only after the Soviet Union detonated its first atomic bomb in 1949 that the situation started to change. Prior to this, the US was the only nation to have fashioned nuclear weapons. They had created the world's first atomic bombs in 1945 and had dropped two of them on Japan right at the end of the war. But now, the Soviets had nuclear weapons of their own.

Even worse, there were reports that the Soviets were also looking into rockets, rockets that could be armed with nuclear warheads. The bombs dropped on Japan would be primitive by comparison. They were simply dropped from planes to land on top of their targets. Being able to put nuclear warheads on top of rockets, or as they would later be called, intercontinental ballistic missiles (ICBMs), would be a real game changer. It was an alarming and sobering thought for Americans, who were quickly feeling the chill of the oncoming Cold War.

As such, it wasn't long before Wernher von Braun was tapped to try and give America the edge in this new and dangerous arms race with Russia. Wernher and his team were relocated to Huntsville, Alabama. Here, in the early 1950s, he developed the so-called Redstone rocket, which was subsequently used for America's first nuclear missiles. By 1953, von Braun was made the chief architect of the program. It was under these auspices that von Braun developed his first Jupiter missile. This missile, although developed for war, would eventually set the stage for the US space program.

From the Jupiter series of missiles came the Juno I rocket that was used to launch the Explorer satellite into orbit on January 31, 1958. This was done in response to the successful launch of the Russian Sputnik satellite during the previous year. The US top brass had become very concerned when the Russians beat them to this technical feat and commissioned Wernher von Braun to help them catch up in what was suddenly becoming not a steady walk toward the stars but an all-out space race.

Chapter Nine

A Cold War and a Space Race

"There is beauty in space, and it is orderly. There is no weather, and there is regularity. It is predictable. Just look at our little Explorer; you can set your clock by it—literally. It is more accurate than your clock. Everything in space obeys the laws of physics. If you know these laws, and obey them, space will treat you kindly."

—Wernher von Braun

Although the start of the Space Race is technically marked by the launching of Russia's Sputnik satellite in 1957, Wernher von Braun had already been preparing for quite some time. He had spent the past few years quietly prepping the public for the idea of space travel. Von Braun figured that if he could generate enough public interest, he could get government contracts from his American benefactors in much the way that the Germans had backed his previous endeavors.

Learning to appreciate America's relative freedom of speech, Wernher von Braun became an outright spokesperson and spoke openly of his aspirations. He even teamed up with none other than Walt Disney himself in 1955 to produce a series of television films about space exploration. Then, in 1959, the year after the successful launch of America's Explorer satellite, Wernher von Braun penned a book on the subject, which particularly emphasized his dream of going to the Moon. This still seemed like fanciful thinking to many back in 1959, but little did they know that in ten short years this objective would be achieved by the Apollo astronauts.

It was on July 29, 1958, in the meantime, that NASA was forged. Shortly thereafter, NASA began building its Marshall Space Flight Center right there in Wernher von Braun's base of Huntsville, Alabama. Von Braun was ultimately made the director of the Marshall Space Flight Center when it opened in 1960. As director, he immediately focused on the development of a heavier launch vehicle he referred to as the Saturn rocket. The proposed design was an upgrade of the previous Jupiter rockets.

It wasn't easy work, and the folks at the newly established NASA had a long road ahead of them, but they were determined to do everything they could to succeed. In order to be successful, they had to pay close attention to every single detail of the rocket launches. This need for meticulousness was clearly indicated in the aftermath of the infamous 4-inch launch—a failed launch that occurred in the fall of 1960. The team had to go over the design as well as the maintenance of the rocket with a fine-toothed comb to figure out what had gone wrong. Their efforts were rewarded when it was discovered that some technician somewhere had messed up and made a prong on a power plug too short. The prong wasn't long enough to properly connect. As a result, the safety system of the rocket detected this uneven voltage and automatically shut the system down as a precaution.

Proving the nature of scientific inquiry is a constant learning process, the team not only learned that a prong was too short but also learned valuable data on the safety system of the rocket and just how reliable it would be in the event of a major malfunction. Taking nothing for granted, Wernher von Braun was indeed concerned with safety, especially when they were preparing the rockets that would eventually carry a human crew. The top brass hoped to have Americans put into space in 1961 before the Russians got there first, but Wernher was so cautious that they were afraid that he was slowing down their progress.

As such, Wernher von Braun would take much of the heat when the Soviets did indeed beat the Americans to the punch, launching their first cosmonaut Yuri Gagarin into orbit on April 12, 1961. The US wasn't far behind since they had American astronaut Alan Shepard up in space less than a month later on May 5, but it still hurt to have the Russians get there before them. This was a race, after all, and the Americans wanted to achieve these significant milestones first.

Wernher von Braun, however, was like the turtle to the Soviet Union's hare, and he was determined that his cautious approach was the slow but steady formula that would ultimately win the Space Race. He was ultimately proven right. The Soviets often rushed things through with very little care about safety protocols and, as a result, had some rather terrible accidents and mishaps. The US, meanwhile, made steady improvements all the way up to the Apollo 11 mission in July 1969. It was this crew of Apollo astronauts who would become the first human beings to step foot on the Moon.

With their first steps onto the lunar surface, they fulfilled Wernher von Braun's childhood ambition and put the Space Race with the Soviet Union to bed.

Conclusion

With his long-time dream of manned spaceflight and landing on the Moon fulfilled, Wernher von Braun retired from NASA on May 26, 1972. Upon his retirement, he and his family relocated to Washington, DC, where he served as a vice president at an aerospace outfit called Fairchild Industries.

It was the following year that Wernher von Braun would pay a routine visit to a doctor, who discovered that he was suffering from kidney cancer. Despite the diagnosis, von Braun was determined to stay active during whatever time he had left. As such, he worked with various pro-space exploration programs, such as the National Space Institute, of which he became the chairman in 1975. He also served on the board of directors for Daimler-Benz in 1976. The following year, however, saw his health take a sharp turn for the worse. The cancer had spread to his pancreas. Wernher von Braun finally passed away on June 16, 1977. He was 65 years old.

Von Braun's legacy is one that continues to evoke both admiration and controversy. As the visionary behind the Apollo missions and the first Moon landing, his work helped to propel humanity into the space age. Yet, his complex past and his affiliation with the Nazi regime remain a point of reflection and debate. While his contributions to space exploration are undeniable, the moral complexities of his legacy continue to spark discussions on the intersection of scientific advancement and ethical responsibility. Ultimately, Wernher von Braun's legacy is a long and complicated one which still continues to be written.

Bibliography

Biddle, Wayne (2012). *Dark Side of the Moon: Wernher von Braun, the Third Reich, and the Space Race*.

Freeman, Marsha (1993). *How we got to the Moon: The Story of the German Space Pioneers*.

Neufeld, Michael J. (2002). *Wernher von Braun, the SS, and Concentration Camp Labor: Questions of Moral, Political, and Criminal Responsibility*.

Spangenburg, Ray & Kit Moser, Diane (2008). *Wernher Von Braun: Rocket Visionary (Makers of Modern Science)*.

Ward, Bob (2005). *Dr. Space: The Life of Wernher Von Braun*.

Weyer, Johannes (2018). *Wernher von Braun*.

Made in the USA
Coppell, TX
11 December 2024

42294841R00038